IT'S ANGRY BIRDS VS BAD PIGGIES IN THE BATTLE OF THE JOKES!

WHO WILL MAKE YOU LAUGH YOUR SOCKS OFF?

WHO WILL MAKE YOU GROAN WITH DESPAIR?

LET THE JOKES COMMENCE!

BIRD BANTER

?

WHICH ANGRY BIRD LOVES BOOKS?
Red.

WHAT DO YOU CALL A GIANT ANGRY BIRD?
A weapon of mass destruction!

WHAT DO YOU CALL AN ANGRY BIRD WITH A HEADACHE?
Level 2.

WHAT DO YOU CALL AN ANGRY BIRD WHO'S JUST HAD AN ANGER MANAGEMENT CLASS?
A bird.

WHAT'S THE BEST MARK A CLEVER BIRD CAN GET AT SCHOOL?
E – for Egg-sellent!

!

WHY DO THE ANGRY BIRDS LOVE DESTRUCTION?
Because it's so egg-citing!

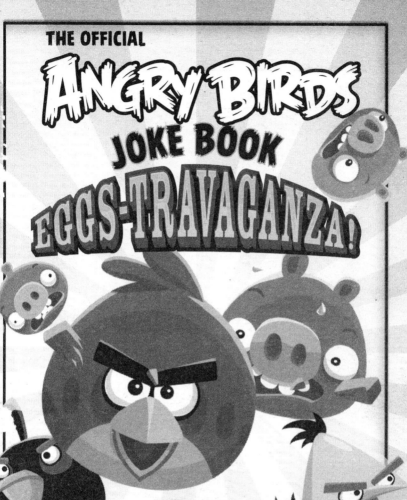

THE OFFICIAL
ANGRY BIRDS
JOKE BOOK
EGGS-TRAVAGANZA!

EGMONT
We bring stories to life

First published in Great Britain 2014 by Egmont UK Limited
The Yellow Building, 1 Nicholas Road, London W11 4AN

ISBN 978 1 4052 7112 7

ANGRY BIRDS

A Side-Splitting, Rib-Tickling Joke Book

WHY ARE THE ANGRY BIRDS BETTER WHEN THEY WORK AS A TEAM?

Because they egg each other on!

WHAT DO YOU GET IF YOU CROSS A TIGER WITH A KANGAROO?

A stripy jumper!

WHAT SOUND DOES AN ANGRY BIRD HEAR WHEN IT FALLS OFF A CLIFF?

An Egg-ho!

WHAT'S YELLOW AND GOES WHEEEEEEEEEEEE-BANG!

Yellow bird.

WHAT DO YOU GET IF YOU CROSS AN ANGRY BIRD WITH A PIG?

Lots of mess!

FEATHERED FROLICS

WHY DON'T DOGS MAKE GOOD DANCERS?

They have two left feet!

WHERE CAN YOU FIND MOZAMBIQUE?

On the Mozam-bird.

WHY DID THE CHICKEN CROSS THE PLAYGROUND?

To get to the other slide.

WHAT DO YOU GET FROM A BAD-TEMPERED SHARK?

As far away as possible!

HOW DO YOU STOP A PIG FROM SMELLING?

Put a peg on its snout!

WHY DON'T POLAR BEARS EAT PENGUINS?

They can't get the wrappers off.

WHAT KIND OF SNAKE IS GOOD AT MATHS?

An adder!

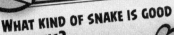

WHY DID THE MUDDY CHICKEN CROSS THE ROAD TWICE?

Because he was a dirty, double crosser!

WHAT DO AN EAGLE AND A LION HAVE IN COMMON?

They both have wings ... except for the lion.

WHAT DO YOU CALL A WOODPECKER WITHOUT A BEAK?

A headbanger.

WHY DID THE PIECE OF CHEWING GUM CROSS THE ROAD?
It was stuck to the chicken's foot!

WHAT DO YOU GET IF YOU RUN OVER A BIRD WITH A LAWNMOWER?
Shredded Tweet.

WHAT DO YOU CALL A GIANT CANARY?
Sir.

WHAT DO YOU CALL A SLEEPING BULL?
A bull-dozer!

WHY DO BIRDS FLY SOUTH FOR THE WINTER?
Because it's too far to walk.

SIDE-SPLITTERS 2

RED BIRD: IF YOU HAD 16 CHOCOLATES AND KING PIG ASKED FOR 10, HOW MANY WOULD YOU HAVE LEFT?

THE BLUE BIRDS: 16. WE DON'T LIKE KING PIG.

HOW DO YOU STOP AN ELEPHANT FROM STAMPEDING?

You take its stampeder away!

WHAT'S THE DIFFERENCE BETWEEN ROAST BEEF AND PEA SOUP?

Anyone can roast beef.

WHAT GOES GREY, YELLOW, GREY, YELLOW, GREY, YELLOW?

An elephant rolling down the hill with a daffodil in its mouth.

WHAT'S A CROCODILE'S FAVOURITE CARD GAME?

Snap!

WHAT DOES A CAT EAT FOR BREAKFAST?

Mice Crispies.

WHERE DO YOU FIND GIANT SNAILS?

At the end of the giant's fingers!

WHAT DO YOU CALL TWO THIEVES?

A pair of nickers!

WHAT FISH ONLY SWIMS AT NIGHT?

A starfish!

CHEEP LAUGHS

WHAT DO YOU CALL A BIRD THAT'S OUT OF BREATH?

A puffin.

WHAT TYPE OF BIRDS SPEND ALL THEIR TIME ON THEIR KNEES?

Birds of prey!

WHAT'S THE BEST TIME TO BUY A BUDGIE?

When it's going cheep!

WHAT DO YOU CALL A RUDE BIRD?

A mockingbird.

WHY IS A CUSHION LIKE A TURKEY?

They both need stuffing.

AVIAN ANTICS

WHAT SOUND DO KISSING HEDGEHOGS MAKE?
Ouch!

WHAT DO YOU GET IF YOU CROSS AN OWL WITH A SKUNK?
A bird that smells, but doesn't give a hoot!

WHAT BIRD STEALS SOAP FROM YOUR BATH?
Robber duck.

WHAT DO YOU CALL A FUNNY DUCK?
A wise quacker.

WHAT'S A POLYGON?
A dead parrot.

WHY CAN'T AN OWL SING IN THE RAIN?
Because it's too wet to woo!

WHAT KIND OF BIRD LIVES UNDERGROUND?

A mynah bird.

WHAT HAPPENED TO THE OWL WHO TRIPPED OVER?

He felt a bit of twit!

WHAT HAPPENED TO THE OWL WHO TRIPPED OVER AFTER THE FIRST OWL?

He felt a bit of twit, twoo!

WHAT DO NAUGHTY BIRDS TURN INTO?

Jail birds.

WHY ARE FISH EASY TO WEIGH?

They have their own scales!

FEATHERBRAINED QUIPS

WHAT BOOKS DO OWLS LIKE?
Hoot-dunnits!

WHAT DID THE POORLY CHICKEN HAVE?
People-pox!

WHICH BIRDS TELL THE BEST JOKES?
Comedi-hens!

WHAT HAS SIX LEGS AND CAN FLY LONG DISTANCES?
Three swallows!

WHAT DO YOU GET IF YOU CROSS A BIRD WITH A FIREWORK?
A Firequacker!

WHY DID THE DUCK MISS HIS TRAIN?

He was doing some last minute quacking!

WHAT IS A PIG'S EXPLANATION FOR THE CREATION OF THE UNIVERSE?

The Pig Bang Theory.

WHY DID THE HEN CROSS THE ROAD, BUT STOP HALF WAY?

She wanted to lay it on the line!

WHO'S THE SMARTEST PIG IN THE WORLD?

Ein-swine

WHY DOES A FLAMINGO LIFT UP ONE LEG?

Because if he lifted up both legs he would fall over!

TROTTER TALES

WHY DO ELEPHANTS NEVER FORGET?
Because no one ever tells them anything!

WHY DID THE CHICKEN GET INTO TROUBLE?
He used fowl language!

WHAT DO PIGS GET ON FEBRUARY 14TH?
Valenswines!

WHAT HAPPENED TO THE CAT WHO SWALLOWED A BALL OF WOOL?
She ended up having mittens!

CHUCKLE TIME

WHY ARE ELEPHANTS SO WRINKLY?
Have you ever tried to iron one?

WHAT KIND OF KEY OPENS A BANANA?
A monkey!

WHAT DID ONE FLEA SAY TO THE OTHER FLEA?
Shall we walk or take the dog?

WHAT'S SMALL AND GREEN AND LIKES TO GO CAMPING?
A boy sprout.

WHAT IS A CROCODILE'S FAVOURITE GAME?
Snap!

REALLY FUNNY JOKES ... HONEST

WHY DO BICYCLES FALL OVER?
Because they are two-tired!

WHY DID THE SNAKE CROSS THE ROAD?
To get to the other sssside!

WHAT DID THE STAMP SAY TO THE ENVELOPE?
Stick with me and we will go places!

WHY COULDN'T THE PIRATE PIG PLAY CARDS?
Because he was sitting on the deck!

WHAT'S SMARTER THAN A TALKING PIG?
A spelling bee!

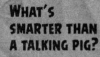

HOGWASH

WHAT IS A PIG'S FAVOURITE BALLET?
Swine Lake!

TWO PIGS IN A STY. ONE SAYS, "OINK!" THE OTHER SAYS, "I WAS GOING TO SAY THAT!"

WHAT'S A PIG'S FAVOURITE GAME?
Backgammon!

HAVE YOU HEARD ABOUT THE PIG WHO TOOK UP DANCING?
He liked to swing his weight around.

DID YOU HEAR OF THE PIG WHO BEGAN HIDING GARBAGE IN NOVEMBER?
She wanted to do her Christmas slopping early that year.

HOGWORDS

WHY DID THE PIGLETS FALL ASLEEP IN CLASS?
Their teacher was a boar!

WHO TOOK 10,000 PIGS UP A HILL?
The grand old Duke of Pork!

WHAT DO YOU GET IF YOU CROSS A DINOSAUR WITH A PIG?
Jurassic Pork.

WHAT DOES A PIG PLAY IN A BAND?
Pigcussion!

WHAT DO YOU CALL A PIG WHO LOVES TO DRIVE?
A road hog!

WHY DID THE PIG EAT ALL THE SOFAS AND CHAIRS?

He thought they were suites!

WHY DID THE PIG EAT THE LAMP?

He wanted a light snack.

WHAT KIND OF NECKWEAR DO PIGS LIKE?

Pig's ties.

WHAT'S A PIG'S FAVOURITE KEY?

Cookies!

HOW DOES A PIG MAKE APPLE CRUMBLE?

He stands on it.

MORE PIGGY FUN

HOW DOES A PIG FEEL WHEN IT LOSES ITS VOICE?

Disgruntled.

IF YOU DROP THIS BOOK IN A PIG PEN, WHAT SHOULD YOU DO?

Take the words out of their mouths.

WHAT DO YOU CALL A PIG ON ROLLERSKATES?

Nothing, just get out of the way!

WHAT DO YOU CALL A PIG LEARNING KARATE?

A pork chop.

WHEN PIGS HAVE A PARTY, WHO JUMPS OUT OF THE CAKE?

Nobody. The pigs all jump in.

GUT-BUSTERS

WHAT DID THE 0 SAY TO THE 8?
Nice belt.

WHERE DO SHEEP GET THEIR HAIR CUT?
At the bah, bah shop.

WHAT DO YOU CALL AN AARDVARK THAT'S AFRAID OF THE DARK?
A Vark.

IF I HAD A NEWT I WOULD CALL HIM TINY, BECAUSE HE WOULD BE MY-NEWT!

?   !

WHAT SPORT DO PIGS ALWAYS GET A GOLD MEDAL IN?
Mud wrestling!

?

WHY IS A TRACTOR MAGIC?
Because it can go down a road and turn into a field!

WHY DID THE SCARECROW WIN AN AWARD?
Because he was out-standing in his field!

WHICH FISH IS THE SLEEPIEST?
A kipper.

WHAT DO YOU CALL A CRAFTY PIG?
Cunningham!

HOW DO YOU STOP YOUR NOSE FROM RUNNING?
Teach it to hop!

PIG PRANKS

WHAT DO PIGS TALK ABOUT?
Hogwash.

HOW DID THE ANGRY BIRDS FIND OUT THE PIGS HAD STOLEN THEIR EGGS?
A piglet squealed on them!

WHAT DO PIGLETS DO AFTER SCHOOL?
Hamwork.

WHAT DO YOU CALL A PIG WITH NO LEGS?
A ground hog!

WHERE DO PIGS EAT THEIR LUNCH?
At a pig-nic table.

WHERE WOULD YOU FIND THEM?
Wherever you left them!

WHAT DO YOU CALL A PIG AT THE END OF LEVEL ONE?

Squashed!

WHAT TIME IS IT WHEN A PIG SITS ON YOUR FENCE?

New fence time!

DID YOU HEAR ABOUT THE PIG WHO TRIED TO START A HOT AIR BALLOON COMPANY?

He couldn't get it off the ground!

WHAT DO YOU GIVE A SICK PIG?

Plenty of room ...

'S ONE SMALL STEP FOR BIRDS, ONE GIANT CHEEP FOR BIRDKIND.

HE ANGRY BIRDS ARE IN SPACE! THEIR MISSION:
O BRING BACK THE BEST JOKES IN THE SOLAR SYSTEM!

HEY BETTER BE QUICK THOUGH ...

HE SPACE PIGS ARE JOKE
UNTING TOO AND THEY ARE
EADY TO BLAST THE BIRDS'
OKES INTO OBLIVION!

SPACE MISSION: GO!

WHAT DO THE ANGRY BIRDS DO WHEN THEY GET REALLY ANGRY IN SPACE?
They blast off!

HOW DO THE ANGRY BIRDS ORGANISE A SPACE MISSION?
They planet.

WHAT DO YOU CALL A SPACESHIP THAT DRIPS WATER?
A crying saucer.

WHY COULDN'T THE ANGRY BIRDS BOOK A ROOM ON THE MOON?
Because it was full.

HOW DID THE ROCKET LOSE ITS JOB?
It was fired!

WHAT DO YOU CALL A PARROT THAT FLEW INTO A BLACK HOLE?
A polygon!

HOW DO THE ANGRY BIRDS PASS THE TIME ON THEIR JOURNEY TO SPACE?
They play Astronauts and Crosses!

WHAT DO YOU CALL AN ALIEN WITH THREE EYES?
An aliiien!

WHAT IS AN ALIEN'S FAVOURITE FOOD?
Martian-mallows!

WHY WAS THE ROBOT ANGRY?
Because somebody kept pushing his buttons!

WHAT'S E.T. SHORT FOR?

Because he's only got little legs.

WHY DID THE ROBOT GO TO THE GARAGE?

Because he had a screw loose!

DO ROBOTS HAVE SISTERS?

No, just tran-sistors!

TWO SATELLITES MET IN SPACE, FELL IN LOVE AND GOT MARRIED. THE CEREMONY WAS RUBBISH, BUT THE RECEPTION WAS BRILLIANT!

PIGGY STARDUST

WHAT IS THE PIGS' EXPLANATION FOR THE CREATION OF THE UNIVERSE?
The Pig Bang Theory!

HOW DO PIGS LAUNCH SPACE SHUTTLES?
By lighting the pig-nition!

WHAT DO YOU CALL A PIG'S MESSY SPACE SHIP?
A pig-sky!

WHAT DO YOU CALL A PIG IN A SPACESUIT?
An astro-snort!

WHY DID THE PIG EAT THE SUN?
He wanted a light snack.

WHAT DID THE PIG THINK OF HIS LONG MISSION TO SPACE?
It was a bit of a boar.

DID YOU HEAR ABOUT THE PIG WHO TRIED TO START A ROCKET BUSINESS?
He couldn't get it off the ground.

WHAT IS A SPACE PIG'S FAVOURITE TV PROGRAMME ABOUT SPACE?
The Sty at Night!

WHO WAS THE FIRST PIG ON THE MOON?
Squeal Armstrong.

PIGGY STARDUST 2

WHY DID THE PIGS PUT EXTRA SEATBELTS ON THEIR SPACE SHUTTLE?

For added sow-curity!

WHAT IS THE PIGS' NICKNAME FOR THEIR LUNAR BUGGY?

Their automo-squeal!

WHAT DID THE PIG SAY WHEN THE ROBOT GRABBED HIS BOTTOM?

This is the end of me!

WHAT DID THE PIGS DO IN THEIR SPACE SHUTTLE?

They all held hams for take-off.

SPACE MUNCH

HOW DID THE ASTRONAUT SERVE DRINKS?

In sunglasses!

WHAT DO THE ANGRY BIRDS EAT IN SPACE?

Mars Bars.

WHERE DO ASTRONAUTS KEEP THEIR LUNCH?

In their launch box!

HOW DO YOU KNOW WHEN THE MOON HAS HAD ENOUGH TO EAT?

When it's full.

WHERE DOES DR WHO BUY HIS CHEESE?

In a dalek-atessen.

FEATHERBRAINED FIREBALLS!

WHAT DO BIRDS FILL THEIR SPACE SHUTTLES WITH?

Rocket fowl!

WHY DID THE BIRDS LAND ON THE WRONG PLANET?

Because they were just winging it!

WHAT DID SUPER RED SAY TO THE ANGRY ROBOT?

Toucan play at this game!

WHAT DID THE ALIEN SAY TO THE ANGRY BIRDS?
You're all raven lunatics!

WHAT DID THE BIRD SAY WHEN IT FLEW OVER A MARTIAN DISCOUNT STORE?
Cheap cheap!

DID THE BIRDS LIKE VENUS?
Yes, they thought it was very pheasant.

HOW DID THE BIRDS DESCRIBE THEIR SMOOTH LANDING ON THE MOON?
Im-peck-able!

HOW LONG WILL THE BIRDS BE IN SPACE?
They are heron 'til Friday.

ASTRO-SNORT LARKS

WHAT DO YOU CALL A CRAZY SPACEMAN?

An astro-nut!

WHAT IS AN ASTRONAUT'S FAVOURITE KEY ON A KEYBOARD?

Space bar!

WHICH ASTRONAUT WEARS THE BIGGEST HELMET?

The one with the biggest head!

WHY DID THE BOY BECOME AN ASTRONAUT?

Because he was no earthly good.

ALIEN ANTICS

WHERE SHOULD A 500-POUND ALIEN GO?

On a diet!

WHY DON'T ALIENS CELEBRATE CHRISTMAS?

Because they don't like to give away their presence.

FIRST ALIEN: IS THERE A PLACE I CAN GET CLEAN?

Second alien: Just go straight ahead and you will see the meteor showers.

WHAT DID THE ALIEN SAY TO THE PETROL PUMP?

Don't you know it's rude to stick your finger in your ear when I'm talking to you?

HOW DOES AN ALIEN COUNT UP TO 25?

On its fingers!

WHAT'S LONG, SLIPPERY AND ALWAYS PHONES HOME WHEN HE GOES SIGHTSEEING?

E.T. – the extra tourist eel.

WHY DON'T ALIENS LIKE CROP CIRCLES?

Because they are so corny!

ROBOTIC RIB-TICKLERS

WHAT DID THE ROBOT SAY TO HIS TEAMMATE BEFORE A FOOTBALL MATCH?
Let's kick some ro-butt!

WHO IS TALL, DARK AND A GREAT DANCER?
Darth Raver!

HOW DO YOU SAY ROBOT BACKWARDS?
Robot backwards.

WHAT DO YOU CALL A ROBOT THAT ALWAYS TAKES THE LONG WAY ROUND?
R2 detour!

HOW DOES A ROBOT SHAVE?
With a laser blade!

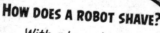

CRASH, BANG, SQUAWK!

WHAT KIND OF SADDLE DO YOU PUT ON A SPACE HORSE?

A saddle-ite!

WHY DID THE SPACE MINION PIGS BANG THEIR HEADS AGAINST THE WALL?

So they would see stars!

HOW DID THE BIRD IN A BROKEN ROCKET GET BACK TO EARTH?

With his sparrow-chute!

WHAT CARTOONS DO MARTIANS WATCH ON TV?
Lunar Tunes!

WHY DID THE PIG'S ROCKET CRASH LAND ON PLUTO?
Because he was only a ham-ateur pilot!

WHY DO ASTRONAUTS WEAR BULLET-PROOF VESTS?
To protect themselves from shooting stars!

SCIENCE SNORTS!

DID YOU HEAR THE ONE ABOUT THE SCIENTIST WHO WAS READING A BOOK ABOUT HELIUM?

He just couldn't put it down!

WHERE DOES BAD LIGHT END UP?

In prism.

WHAT DO YOU GET IF YOU CROSS A STUDENT AND AN ALIEN?

Something from another universe-ity!

WHY DID THE PIG SIT ON THE COMPUTER?

To keep an eye on the mouse!

HOW DO COMPUTERS MAKE JUMPERS?

On the inter-knit!

SNOUT-RAGEOUS SOLAR SIZZLERS

HOW CAN YOU MAKE YOUR MONEY GO FURTHEST?

Put your piggy bank in a rocket!

WHERE DO PIGS LOOK FOR STARS?

Up in the sty, of course.

WHAT DO YOU GET IF YOU CROSS SANTA CLAUS WITH A SPACE SHIP?

A U-F-Ho-Ho-Ho!

WHAT DID THE PIG ASTRONAUT SAY BEFORE HIS ROCKET LAUNCH?

Let's hope for swill weather.

WHY IS THE MOON BALD?
It has no air!

HOW DID THE BIRD MAKE CONTACT WITH HIS FRIENDS FROM SPACE?
By making a long-distance telephone caw.

WHY DO THE SPACE MINION PIGS SOMETIMES FLY THROUGH SPACE WITH THEIR EYES SHUT?
Because they know the universe inside snout.

HOW DO YOU GREET A TWO-HEADED ALIEN?
Hello, hello!

COSMIC ANIMAL CRACKERS

WHAT'S THE DIFFERENCE BETWEEN A PIG'S TAIL AND LAUNCHING A ROCKET AT 6AM?
Nothing, they're both twirly!

HOW DID THE COW JUMP OVER THE MOON?
It flew through udder space!

HOW DID THE BIRDS TELL EVERYONE ON EARTH THEY HAD LANDED ON MARS?
They sent a tweet!

WHY DID THE COW GO TO SPACE?
Because it wanted to visit the mooooooooon!

WHAT DO ALIEN CATS HAVE FOR BREAKFAST?

A flying saucer of milk.

HOW DID THE DOG STOP THE ROCKET CRASHING INTO THE SUN?

By pressing the paws button!

WHY DID THE COW GO TO OUTER SPACE?

To visit the Milky Way!

WHY DID THE DOG VISIT MARS?

To see if there was an alien pup-ulation!

TWEETING TICKLERS

WHAT ARE THE BIRDS PROTECTING IN SPACE?

Eggs-teroids!

WHAT DID THE FIRST BIRD TO LAND ON THE MOON SAY?

One small peck for birds, one giant cheep for birdkind.

WHY DID THE BIRDS GO UP TO SPACE TO SING?

So they could reach the high notes.

WHAT GAME DO THE ANGRY BIRDS PLAY IN SPACE?

Moon-opoly!.

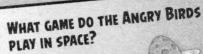

HOW DOES AN ALIEN TRIM A BIRD'S FEATHERS?

Eclipse them!

WHAT DID THE ANGRY BIRD COOK IN SPACE?

An unidentified frying object!

ALIEN ANTICS PART 2

HOW CAN YOU TELL IF AN ALIEN HAS USED YOUR TOOTHBRUSH?

It glows in the dark!

WHAT'S AN ALIEN'S NORMAL EYESIGHT?

20-20-20

HOW DOES AN ALIEN CONGRATULATE SOMEONE?

They give a high six.

WHY SHOULDN'T YOU INSULT AN ALIEN?

You might hurt its feelers.

WHY DO ASTRONAUTS LIKE TO DO SUBTRACTION?

They're always ready to countdown.

WHY DID THE ASTRONAUT PUT WHEELS ON HIS ROCKING CHAIR?

He wanted to rock 'n' roll!

IF ASTRONAUTS ARE SO SMART, WHY DO THEY COUNT BACKWARDS?

HOW DO ASTRONAUTS KEEP THEIR ROCKETS FREE FROM DUST?

They drive through the vacuum of outer space!

3
2
1
BLAST OFF!
HOW DID THE ASTRONAUT SAY SORRY TO HIS FRIEND?
He apollo-gised!
I WANT TO BE AN ASTRONAUT WHEN I GROW UP.
What high hopes you have!
WHAT HAPPENS TO ASTRONAUTS THAT MISBEHAVE?
They're grounded!

THE GREEDY PIGGIES' SPACE MOVIES

E.T. THE EGGSTRA-TERRESTRIAL

THE RETURN OF THE BODY-SNACKERS

WALL-PEA

THE MEAT-RIX

MASH GORDON

MEN IN SNACK

THUNDERBIRDS ARE DOUGH!
INDEPENDENCE SUNDAE
THE RETURN OF THE JELLY
FLY ME TO THE PRUNE
EGGS MEN
SCONE WARS

STY ME TO THE MOON

WHAT KIND OF BULBS DID THE ANGRY BIRDS PLANT ON THE MOON?

Light bulbs!

WHY DO THE STARS COME OUT AT NIGHT?

They have nowhere else to go.

DID YOU HEAR THE ONE ABOUT THE TWO GREEN ALIENS AND THE SPACESHIP?

It was out of this world!

ALIEN INVASION!

WHY DO ALIENS TICKLE YOU BEFORE A MEAL?

They like a happy meal!

DID YOU HEAR ABOUT THE ALIEN THAT THREW AWAY HIS TRAINERS BECAUSE THEY WERE STICKING THEIR TONGUES OUT AT HIM?

WHAT ALIEN HAS EIGHT LEGS, TWO BOTTOMS, FIVE ARMS, TEN EYES, BLACK TEETH AND A SNOTTY NOSE?

An extremely ugly one!

DOUBLE CROSSING

WHAT DO YOU GET IF YOU CROSS A PIG WITH THE FIRST MAN ON THE MOON?

Neil Hamstring!

WHAT DO YOU GET IF YOU CROSS AN OWL WITH A TIME LORD?

Dr Hoo Woo!

WHAT DO YOU GET IF YOU CROSS A FLUFFY BIRD WITH A METEOR SHOWER?

Fowl weather!

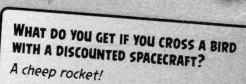

WHAT DO YOU GET IF YOU CROSS A BIRD WITH A DISCOUNTED SPACECRAFT?

A cheep rocket!

WHAT DO YOU GET IF YOU CROSS A FURRY BIRD WITH A SPACE RANGER?

Fuzz Lightyear!

HOW DID THE NAUGHTY BIRD GET OUT OF SPACE PRISON?
He made a great egg-scape!

WHAT IS THE MOST DANGEROUS THING IN SPACE?
A shooting star!

HOW DO YOU CATCH A UNIQUE ALIEN?
Unique up on it!

WHAT SHOULD THE PIGS LOOK OUT FOR WHEN THEY VISIT STRANGE PLANETS?

Pig-pockets!

WHAT SHOULD YOU DO IF AN ALIEN SPACESHIP CRASHES INTO YOUR FRONT DOOR?

Run out through the back door!

WHY DID THE BIRD HAVE TO PAY A FINE?

It broke the law of gravity!

GRUB BUSTERS!

WHAT IS A PIG'S FAVOURITE KIND OF PARTY?
A cheese and swine party!

WHAT DID THE PIG EAT WITH HIS PASTA IN SPACE?
Dalek bread!

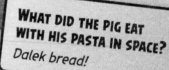

HOW DID THE ROBOT GET AN ELECTRIC SHOCK?
He stood on a bun and a currant ran up his leg!

WHEN DO MARTIANS EAT EYEBALLS?

On fried-eyes!

WHAT'S GREEN AND SQUIRTS JAM AT YOU?

A alien eating a donut!

WHAT WAS THE FIRST COFFEE BAR IN SPACE?

Starbucks!

WHY DID THE PIG FEED THE CHICKEN WHISKY?

He wanted scotch eggs!

MARTIAN MADNESS

WHAT HAPPENED TO THE FUNNY MARTIAN WHO ATE AN OXO CUBE?

He made a laughing stock out of himself!

WHAT IS ZOG THE MARTIAN'S MIDDLE NAME?

The.

WHAT DO YOU DO WITH A BLUE MARTIAN?

Try to cheer him up.

WHAT DO YOU CALL A FLEA WHO LIVES IN A MARTIAN'S EAR?
A space invader!

WHY ARE MARTIANS GREEN?
Because they forget to take their travel sickness pills!

DID YOU HEAR ABOUT THE SILLY MARTIAN WHO BOUGHT A SLEEPING BAG?
He spent two weeks trying to wake it up!

MORE MARTIAN MADNESS

DID YOU HEAR ABOUT THE MARTIAN WHO HAD A FACE LIKE A MILLION DOLLARS?
It was green and wrinkled!

WHY ARE MARTIANS SO GOOD AT WEEDING?
Because they have green fingers!

WHAT DO YOU GET IF YOU CROSS A MARTIAN WITH A COW?
Milkshakes that are out of this world!

WHERE DO MARTIANS PLAY FOOTBALL?
On Astro-turf!

COSMIC MISH-MASH!

WHY DID THE ANGRY BIRDS THROW THEIR CLOCK OUT OF THEIR SPACESHIP?

They wanted to see time fly.

WHY DID THE ROBOT CROSS THE ROAD?

It was programmed by the chicken!

WHY WOULDN'T THE PIG LET SATURN USE HIS BATH?

Because he'd leave a ring around it!

HOW MANY EARS DID THE SCI-FI FAN HAVE?

Three. A left ear, a right ear and a final front ear!

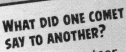
WHAT DID ONE COMET SAY TO ANOTHER?
Pleased to meteor.

WHAT ILLNESS DO RETIRED ASTRONAUT BIRDS GET?
Flew.

WHAT HAS A GREEN AND YELLOW STRIPED BODY, SIX HAIRY LEGS AND GREAT BIG EYES ON STALKS?

I don't know, Why?

ONE HAS JUST CRAWLED OUT OF YOUR SPACE SUIT!

WHY ARE ROTTEN TEETH LIKE OUTER SPACE?

They're full of black holes.

WHAT'S GREEN AND COUGHS?

A Martian with a cold.

WHAT'S GREEN AND GOES ROUND AND ROUND AT 60 MPH?

A Martian in a blender!

WHAT DO YOU GET IF YOU CROSS A MARTIAN'S NOSE WITH A GOLF COURSE?

A little green bogey.

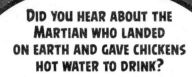

HOW MANY ASTRONAUTS DOES IT TAKE TO CHANGE A LIGHTBULB?

None! Astronauts aren't afraid of the dark!

WHAT HAPPENED TO THE ASTRONAUT WHO REACHED THE MOON IN FIVE MINUTES FLAT?

She got into the Guinness Book of Out-Of-This-World Records.

WHAT KIND OF CAR DOES A SCI-FI FAN DRIVE?

A toy-yoda.

IF A FLYING SAUCER IS A SPACECRAFT, WHAT IS A BROOMSTICK?

Witchcraft.

I WAS UP ALL NIGHT WONDERING WHERE THE SUN HAD GONE.

Then it dawned on me ...

WHY DID THE PLANET GET KICKED OUT OF SCHOOL?

It kept mooning at the class!

WHAT DID THE SPACE PIGS SAY WHEN THEY FOUND OUT SUPER RED HAD PUT CANDYFLOSS IN THE ENGINE OF THEIR SPACESHIP?

I think there's been some fowl play here!

EARTH IS CAW-LING!

WHAT DID THE BIRD SAY TO THE ALIEN BURGLAR ON EARTH?

Don't be robin anything from our planet!

TWO ALIENS WALKED INTO A GAMES ARCADE ON EARTH. "GOODNESS," SAID ONE, STARING AROUND IN AMAZEMENT. "PEOPLE HERE FEED THEIR PETS WITH METAL DISKS!"

WHAT DID THE BIRD SAY WHEN SHE GOT BACK FROM HER MISSION TO SPACE?

It's the best place I've feather been!

WHAT IS THE CENTRE OF GRAVITY?

The letter V.

DO YOU THINK EARTH MAKES FUN OF MARS FOR HAVING NO LIFE?

WHAT DID THE MOTHER ALIEN SAY TO THE CHILD ALIEN?

Where on Earth have you been?

WHILE LIVING ON EARTH MIGHT BE EXPENSIVE, AT LEAST YOU GET A FREE TRIP AROUND THE SUN EVERY YEAR!

WHO IS THE CLEVEREST PIG ON EARTH?

Swine-stein.

WHAT IS AT THE END OF THE WORLD?

The letter D.

SILLY SPACE TICKLERS

WHY DID THE ALIEN SLEEP UNDER THE LEAKING SPACESHIP?
He wanted to wake up oily!

WHY DID THE MARTIAN ORDER A DOUBLE BURGER?
He wanted a meteor meal!

MISSION TO LAND

THE ANGRY BIRDS HAVE LANDED BACK ON EARTH! THEIR MISSION TO FIND THE BEST JOKES IN THE UNIVERSE IS OVER. SO, WHAT DID THEY THINK OF LIFE IN SPACE?

"IT WAS QUITE A **BIRD-EN** TO MAKE IT THROUGH THE WORMHOLE SAFELY. I DON'T **WREN-COMMEND** IT FOR EVERYONE BUT **OWL** JUST SAY HOW **EGG-CITING** IT IS UP THERE!"

PHEW! YOU MADE IT THROUGH THE ANGRY BIRDS' SPACE MISSION IN ONE PIECE! IS YOUR BELLY ACHING YET? NO? WELL LET'S TAKE A RIB-TICKLING TRIP THROUGH THE SEASONS TO REALLY GET THOSE TEARS ROLLING!

DON'T SAY YOU WEREN'T WARNED ...

VALEN-SWINE'S DAY

WHY DID THE PIG GIVE HIS GIRLFRIEND A BOX OF CHOCOLATES?

It was Valen-swine's Day!

WHAT DID THE STAMP SAY TO THE ENVELOPE ON VALENTINE'S DAY?

I'm stuck on you!

WHAT DID THE BOY BIRD SAY TO THE GIRL BIRD ON VALENTINE'S DAY?

Let me call you tweet-heart!

WHY DID THE BANANA GO OUT WITH THE PRUNE?

Because it couldn't get a date.

WHAT DID THE OVERWEIGHT PIG SAY TO HIS GIRLFRIEND?

I love you a ton!

KNOCK, KNOCK!
Who's there?
OLIVE.
Olive who?
OLIVE YOU, TOO!

WHAT DID THE BOY SQUIRREL SAY TO THE GIRL SQUIRREL ON VALENTINE'S DAY?
I'm nuts about you!

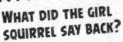

WHAT DID THE GIRL SQUIRREL SAY BACK?
You're nuts so bad yourself!

WHY DOESN'T BOMB LIKE TALKING TO GIRLS?
He's worried there'd be a spark between them!

WHAT KIND OF DATE DOES CHUCK LIKE TO GO ON?
Speed dating!

HOGS AND KISSES 2

WHAT DID THE CHOCOLATE SYRUP SAY TO THE ICE CREAM?

I'm sweet on you!

WHAT HAPPENED TO THE COUPLE WHO MET IN A REVOLVING DOOR?

They're still going around together!

WHY DID MINION PIG BREAK UP WITH HIS GIRLFRIEND?

He was green with envy!

HOW DID THE TELEPHONE PROPOSE TO HIS GIRLFRIEND?

He gave her a ring.

WHAT DID ONE LIGHT BULB SAY TO THE OTHER?

I love you a whole watt!

WHY DID MINION PIG HAVE HIS GIRLFRIEND PUT IN JAIL?

She stole his heart.

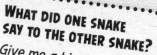

WHAT DID ONE SNAKE SAY TO THE OTHER SNAKE?
Give me a hiss!

WHAT DID ONE FISH SAY TO THE OTHER FISH?
You're quite a catch!

WHAT DID RED SAY TO KING PIG?
Watch out, I'm about to get a crush on you!

KNOCK, KNOCK!
Who's there?
HOWARD.
Howard who?
HOWARD YOU LIKE A GREAT BIG KISS?

YEAR OF THE DRAGON

HOW DID THE DRAGON WIN THE TALENT CONTEST?
She was the beast in the show!

WHAT DO YOU DO WITH A GREEN DRAGON?
Wait until it ripens!

WHAT DO THE PIGS THINK OF MIGHTY DRAGON?
He makes them sizzle!

WHERE DID THE DRAGON LEARN TO BREATHE FIRE?
At knight school!

WHAT'S PURPLE, 10,000 KM LONG AND 12 M HIGH?
The grape wall of China.

WHAT DID THE DRAGON SAY WHEN HE
SAW A KNIGHT IN SHINING ARMOUR?
Oh no, not more tinned food!

WHY DID THE DRAGON
CROSS THE ROAD?
Because he'd scared
away all the chickens!

THE BLUES
WON'T GO
TO SCHOOL!

They'll go,
even if I end up
dragon them
there myself!

WHAT DO YOU DO WHEN
A DRAGON SNEEZES?
Get out of the way!

WHAT DID THE DRAGON SAY
TO THE PIECE OF BREAD?
You're toast!

YEAR OF THE DRAGON 2

WHAT'S BLACK AND WHITE AND GOES ROUND AND ROUND?

A panda stuck in a revolving door.

WHAT DO CHINESE DRAGONS EAT FOR BREAKFAST?

Panda-cakes!

KNOCK, KNOCK,

Who's there?

DRAGON.

Dragon who?

STOP DRAGON YOUR FEET AND OPEN THE DOOR!

WHY DO DRAGONS SLEEP DURING THE DAY?

So they can fight knights.

SILLY SPRING!

WHEN DO MONKEYS FALL FROM THE SKY?
During Ape-ril showers!

WHY DID RED GO TO THE HOSPITAL?
He needed tweetment!

WHY IS EVERYONE SO TIRED ON APRIL 1ST?
Because they've just finished a 31 day March!

WHICH FLOWER GROWS UNDER YOUR NOSE?
Tulips!

WHY DID THE CHICK DISAPPOINT HIS MOTHER?
He wasn't what he was cracked up to be.

WHAT DO YOU CALL A LAMB WITH NO LEGS?

A cloud.

WHAT DID THE OWL SAY IN THE SPRING SHOWER?

"Too-wet-to-woo!"

CAN FEBRUARY MARCH?

No, but April May!

HOW MANY LAMBS DOES IT TAKE TO KNIT A SWEATER?

Don't be silly – lambs can't knit!

WHY IS THE LETTER A LIKE A FLOWER?

Because a B comes after it!

WHAT DO YOU GET IF YOU CROSS A BOA CONSTRICTOR AND A SHEEP?

A wrap-around jumper!

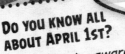

DO YOU KNOW ALL ABOUT APRIL 1ST?

Yes, I'm fool-y aware of it!

HOPPITY SLOP!

WHAT DO YOU CALL A GIRL WITH A FROG ON HER HEAD?

Lily!

HOW DO YOU KNOW CARROTS ARE GOOD FOR YOUR EYES?

Because you never see a rabbit wearing glasses!

WHY DID THE BUNNY BUILD HERSELF A NEW HOUSE?

She was fed up with the hole thing.

WHAT DID THE RABBIT GIVE HIS GIRLFRIEND?

A 14 carrot ring!

DID YOU HEAR ABOUT THE RICH RABBIT?

He was a million-hare!

WHAT IS A RABBIT'S FAVORITE DANCE STYLE?

Hip hop!

BLOOMING PORKERS

HOW DO TREES GET ON THE INTERNET?
They log on!

WHY IS KING PIG LIKE A FLOWER?
He rose to power!

I JUST BOUGHT A NEW BOOK ON GARDENING.

Why?

BECAUSE I WANT TO BE A GOOD WEEDER!

EGGS-CITING EASTER

WHY IS THE EASTER BUNNY SO CLEVER?

He's an egghead!

WHY COULDN'T THE EASTER EGG FAMILY WATCH TV?

Because their signal was scrambled.

HOW LONG DO THE ANGRY BIRDS WORK ON EASTER SUNDAY?

Around the cluck!

WHAT DO YOU CALL A SLEEPY ANGRY BIRD?

Eggs-austed!

HOW SHOULD YOU SEND A LETTER TO THE EASTER BUNNY?

By hare mail!

WHERE DOES THE EASTER BUNNY GET HIS EGGS?

From Eggplants!

WHAT'S LONG, STYLISH AND FULL OF CATS?

The Easter Purr-rade!

DID YOU HEAR ABOUT THE FARMER WHO FED CRAYONS TO HIS CHICKENS?

He wanted them to lay colourful eggs for Easter!

WHY DO PEOPLE PAINT EASTER EGGS?

Because it's easier than wallpapering them!

THERE WAS A ROOSTER SITTING ON A TOP OF A BARN. IF IT LAID AN EGG, WHICH WAY WOULD IT ROLL?

Roosters don't lay eggs!

HOW DO THE ANGRY BIRDS FIND THEIR PRECIOUS EGGS?

Eggs mark the spot!

ST. PATRICK'S DAY HONKERS

WHY DO PEOPLE WEAR SHAMROCKS ON ST. PATRICK'S DAY?

Because real rocks are too heavy.

WHY SHOULDN'T YOU IRON A FOUR-LEAF CLOVER?

Because you don't want to press your luck.

KNOCK, KNOCK!

Who's there?

IRISH.

Irish Who?

IRISH YOU A HAPPY ST. PATRICK'S DAY!

ARE PEOPLE JEALOUS OF THE IRISH?

Sure, they're green with envy!

WHAT WOULD YOU GET IF YOU CROSSED CHRISTMAS WITH ST. PATRICK'S DAY?

St. O'Claus!

WHY ARE LEPRECHAUNS SO HARD TO GET ALONG WITH?
Because they're very short-tempered!

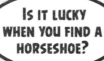

IS IT LUCKY WHEN YOU FIND A HORSESHOE?

Not for the horse!

HOW IS A BEST FRIEND LIKE A FOUR-LEAF CLOVER?
Because they are hard to find and lucky to have.

WHY IS A RIVER ALWAYS LUCKY WITH MONEY?
It has two banks!

WHY DO LEPRECHAUNS MAKE GOOD JOURNALISTS?
They're great at shorthand!

FOUR CHEEP CLOVER

WHY CAN'T YOU BORROW MONEY FROM A LEPRECHAUN?
Because they are always a little short.

WHO'S THE LUCKIEST ANGRY BIRD?
The one at the end of the queue!

WHY DO PIGS HIDE BEHIND FOUR-LEAF CLOVERS?
They need all the luck they can get!

SIZZLING SUMMER SIDE-SPLITTERS!

WHERE DO RETIRED PIGS GO IN THE SUMMER?
To the tro-pigs!

WHERE DOES A SHIP GO WHEN IT'S SICK?
To the dock!

WHAT DO YOU CALL A BIRD WHO IS OUT OF BREATH IN THE HOT SUN?
A puffin!

WHAT'S THE BEST DAY TO GO TO THE BEACH?
Sun-day!

WHY DO FISH SWIM IN SALT WATER?
Because pepper makes them sneeze!

WHY ARE GULLS NAMED SEAGULLS?
If they were in the bay, they'd be bagels!

WHY DID THE TEACHER WEAR SUNGLASSES?
Because his class was so bright!

WHAT DOES A POTATO DO WHEN IT'S HOT?
Take off its jacket!

WHY DO BANANAS USE SUNCREAM?
Because they peel!

WHAT DO WHALES EAT WITH ICE CREAM?
Jellyfish!

WHY DID THE PIG GO ON HOLIDAY ON HIS OWN?
Because all his friends at home were taking him for grunted!

WHERE DOES A FISH GO TO BORROW MONEY?
A loan shark!

HOLIDAY TWEETS!

HOW DID THE BIRD CRASH-LAND ON THE DESERT ISLAND?

With its sparrow-chute!

WHAT'S BLACK, WHITE AND RED ALL OVER?

A penguin with sunburn!

HOW DO SAILORS WASH THEIR CLOTHES?

They throw their laundry overboard and it's washed ashore!

WHAT'S A GOOD HOLIDAY TIP?
Never catch snowflakes in your mouth until the birds have flown south for the winter!

WHAT FLIES THROUGH THE JUNGLE SINGING OPERA?
The parrots of Penzance.

HOW DO CROWS STICK TOGETHER IN A FLOCK?
Vel-crow!

SUMMER PIG-NICS

WHERE DO PIGS EAT THEIR PICNICS IN NEW YORK?

Central Pork!

WHAT DO YOU CALL A DOG ON THE BEACH IN SUMMER?

A hot dog!

WHERE DO THE PIGS GO ON HOLIDAY?

The Cook Islands

WHAT DID THE PIG SAY ON A HOT DAY?

I'm bacon!

WHAT'S THE BEST TYPE OF FOOD TO EAT TO KEEP COOL?

Chilli!

WHERE CAN YOU LEARN HOW TO MAKE ICE CREAM?

At sundae school.

WHERE DO DOGS GO ON HOLIDAY?

A theme bark!

WHAT DO THE ANGRY BIRDS GET IN A HEATWAVE?

Boiled eggs!

KNOCK, KNOCK!

Who's there?

ICE CREAM SODA.

Ice cream soda who?

ICE CREAM SODA PEOPLE CAN HEAR ME!

HOW DO YOU GET A FISH TO KEEP A SECRET?

Ask it not to tell a sole!

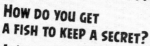

HAPPY BIRD-DAY

WHAT DID THE PIG SAY WHEN HE OPENED HIS BIRTHDAY PRESENT?

That snout my style.

WHAT'S A PARROT'S FAVOURITE BIRTHDAY GAME?

Hide and speak!

WHAT DOES EVERY BIRTHDAY END WITH?

y!

WHAT DO YOU ALWAYS GET ON YOUR BIRTHDAY?

Another year older!

WHAT DID THE ELEPHANT WISH FOR ON HIS BIRTHDAY?

A trunk full of gifts!

WHAT IS A PIG'S FAVOURITE TYPE OF PARTY?

A sow-prize party!

WHAT DID ONE CANDLE SAY TO THE OTHER?

Don't birthdays burn you up?

HAL: I get heartburn every time I eat birthday cake.

RED: Next time don't eat the candles!

WHAT GOES UP AND NEVER COMES DOWN?

Your age!

KNOCK, KNOCK.

Who's there?

ABBY.

Abby who?

ABBY BIRTHDAY!

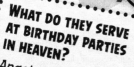

WHAT DO THEY SERVE AT BIRTHDAY PARTIES IN HEAVEN?

Angel cake, of course!

WHAT DO YOU GIVE A 900-POUND GORILLA FOR HIS BIRTHDAY?

I don't know, but you'd better hope he likes it!

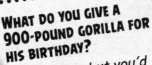

AUTUMNAL ANTICS

WHAT DID THE BIRD SAY WHEN ALL THE LEAVES TURNED GOLD AND RED?

This is very pheasant!

WHAT DID ONE LEAF SAY TO ANOTHER?

I'm falling for you.

WHY DID THE PIG CUT A HOLE IN HIS UMBRELLA?

He wanted to be able to tell when it had stopped raining!

THE BIRDS DON'T LIKE WEARING RAINCOATS... THEY'VE GOT ANORAK-NAPHOBIA!

WHAT ALWAYS FALLS DOWN IN AUTUMN?

Leaves!

WHAT DID THE BIRD SAY WHEN SHE SAW A BIG OAK TREE?

"That's probably the best tree I have feather seen."

WHAT DID THE BEAVER SAY TO THE TREE?
It's been nice gnawing you!

WHAT DID THE TREE WEAR TO THE POOL PARTY?
Swimming trunks!

WHAT IS A TREE'S LEAST FAVOURITE MONTH?
Sep-timber!

WHY DID THE LEAF GO TO THE DOCTOR?
It was feeling green!

WHAT KIND OF TREE CAN FIT INTO YOUR HAND?
A palm tree!

WHAT IS GREEN AND PECKS ON TREES?
Woody Wood-pickle!

MORE AUTUMNAL ANTICS

WHAT DID THE BIRD SAY TO HER FRIEND WHEN SHE NEEDED HELP COLLECTING BERRIES?

Can you sparrow a minute?

HOW CAN YOU TELL THAT A TREE IS A DOGWOOD TREE?

By its bark!

WHAT KIND OF PANTS DO CLOUDS PUT ON?

Thunder-wear!

WHAT FALLS BUT NEVER HITS THE GROUND?

The temperature!

WHAT DID THE CLOUD SAY TO THE LIGHTNING BOLT?

You're shocking!

WHEN DOES IT RAIN MONEY?

When there's a change in the weather.

WHO DOES EVERYONE LISTEN TO, BUT NO ONE BELIEVES?

The weatherman.

DID YOU HEAR THE ONE ABOUT THE OAK TREE?

It's a-corny one!

WHAT DO YOU CALL IT WHEN IT RAINS CHICKENS AND DUCKS?

Foul weather!

WHAT DID THE BIRD SAY WHEN HE WAS ASKED TO MIGRATE TO AUSTRALIA?

That's ostrich too far.

BACK TO SCHOOL!

WHO'S THE LEADER OF SCHOOL STATIONERY?

The ruler!

WHAT KIND OF SCHOOL DOES A SURFER GO TO?

Boarding school!

WHAT KIND OF SCHOOL DOES A GIANT GO TO?

High school!

HOW CAN YOU MAKE SO MANY MISTAKES IN JUST ONE DAY?

I get up early!

WHAT'S THE DIFFERENCE BETWEEN A TEACHER AND A TRAIN?

A teachers says "Spit out your gum!" and a train says "Chew! Chew!"

WHAT WOULD HAPPEN IF YOU TOOK THE SCHOOL BUS HOME?

The headmaster would make you bring it back!

WHY DID THE STUDENT THROW HIS WATCH OUT OF THE WINDOW?

He wanted to see time fly.

WHY IS A MATHS BOOK ALWAYS UNHAPPY?

Because it has a lot of problems!

WHAT DID THE PIGS DO AFTER SCHOOL?

Ham-work!

WHY DID THE STUDENT TAKE A LADDER TO SCHOOL?

He wanted to get a higher education!

HAM'O'WEEN

HOW DO YOU FIX A BROKEN PUMPKIN?

With a pumpkin patch!

WHAT IS A VAMPIRE'S SWEETHEART CALLED?

His ghoul-friend!

WHAT DO YOU GET IF YOU CROSS A SNOWMAN WITH A VAMPIRE?

Frostbite!

WHAT DID THE MUMMY SAY TO THE DETECTIVE?

Let's wrap this case up!

WHY DID THE VAMPIRES HAVE TO CANCEL THEIR GAME OF CRICKET?

Because they couldn't find their bats!

WHAT'S THE SPOOKIEST MATHS PROBLEM?

Pumpkin Pi!

HOW DO MONSTERS TELL THEIR FUTURE?

They read their horror-scope!

WHAT DID THE PIGS SERVE AT THEIR HALLOWEEN PARTY?

I scream!

WHY DON'T MUMMIES HAVE HOBBIES?

Because they're too wrapped up in their work!

WHY DID THE CYCLOPS GIVE UP TEACHING?

Because he only had one pupil!

ANGRY BIRD: What are you dressed up as?

OWL: You figure it hoot.

FRIGHT NIGHT!

WHAT SHOULD YOU DO WHEN ZOMBIES SURROUND YOUR HOUSE?

Hope it's Halloween!

WHAT DO YOU CALL A WITCH AT THE BEACH?

A sand-witch.

WHAT DO THE ANGRY BIRDS LIKE TO DO ON HALLOWEEN?

Go trick or tweeting!

WHAT HAPPENED WHEN THE YOUNG WITCH MISBEHAVED?

She was sent to her broom.

WHERE DO GHOSTS BUY THEIR FOOD?

The ghost-ery store!

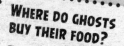

WHAT DO WITCHES PUT ON THEIR HAIR?

Scare-spray!

WHY DO PIGS LOVE HALLOWEEN?

There's lots of hogs gobblin'!

WHY IS A WITCH LIKE AN ANGRY BIRD?

They both like to fly off the handle!

WHERE DO PIGS LIKE TO GO TRICK OR TREATING?

In their neigh-boar hood!

WHERE DO ZOMBIES LIKE TO GO SWIMMING?

The Dead Sea!

WHAT MAKES A SKELETON LAUGH?

When someone tickles its funny bone!

FRIGHT NIGHT PART 2

WHY DID THE MUMMY FEEL TENSE?

He was all wound up!

WHEN DOES A GHOST LIKE TO HAVE BREAKFAST?

In the moaning.

WHAT KIND OF ROADS DO GHOSTS HAUNT?

Dead ends.

WHAT DO BABY GHOSTS WEAR ON THEIR FEET?

Boo-ties!

WHY CAN'T SKELETONS HELP THE ANGRY BIRDS DEFEAT THE PIGS?

They have no guts!

WHAT DID THE PIG WEAR TO DRESS UP AS A VAMPIRE?

Ma-scare-a!

WHERE DO BABY GHOSTS GO?

Day-scare!

WHY DID THE HEADLESS HORSEMAN GO INTO BUSINESS?

He wanted to get ahead in life!

WHAT DO GHOSTS EAT FOR BREAKFAST?

Spook-ghetti!

WHERE DO GHOSTS LIKE TO PARTY?

Anywhere they can boo-gie!

WHAT IS DRACULA'S LEAST-FAVOURITE SONG?

You are my sunshine!

WHAT INSTRUMENT DO SKELETONS PLAY?

The trombone!

WHAT'S IT LIKE TO BE BITTEN BY A VAMPIRE?

A bit of a pain in the neck!

WHY DOES DRACULA TAKE COLD MEDICINE?

He can't stop coffin!

WHAT IS A WITCH'S BEST SUBJECT AT SCHOOL?

Spelling!

HAPPY BIRD-DAY ONCE MORE!

RED: I guess I didn't get my birthday wish.

KING PIG: How do you know?

RED: You're still here!

WHERE DO YOU FIND A BIRTHDAY PRESENT FOR A CAT?

In a cat-alogue!

HOW CAN YOU TELL IF AN ELEPHANT HAS BEEN TO YOUR BIRTHDAY PARTY?

Look for his footprints in the ice cream.

WHERE DOES A SNOWMAN PUT HIS BIRTHDAY CANDLES?

On his birthday flake!

WHAT DID THE BIG CANDLE SAY TO THE LITTLE CANDLE?

You're too young to go out!

WINTER TICKLERS

WHAT DO YOU CALL A BIRD IN WINTER?

A brrrr-d!

WHAT'S AN IG?

A snow house without a loo!

IF THIS SNOW GETS ANY WORSE WE'RE ALL JUST GOING TO HAVE TO GRIT OUR TEETH!

WHAT EIGHT LETTERS CAN YOU FIND IN COLD WATER?

H to O!

KNOCK, KNOCK!

Who's there?

EMMA!

Emma who?

EMMA BIT COLD OUT HERE – LET ME IN!

WHY DO THE PIGS LOVE ICY WEATHER?

It makes it easier for them to slip away!

WHAT DID THE BIG FURRY HAT SAY TO THE WARM WOOLLY SCARF?

You hang around while I go on ahead.

WHY DO BIRDS FLY SOUTH IN WINTER?

Because it's too far to walk!

WHAT DO YOU CALL A REINDEER WITH NO EYES?

I have no eye deer.

WHAT VEGETABLE WAS FORBIDDEN ON THE SHIPS OF ARCTIC EXPLORERS?

Leeks!

WHY DOES IT TAKE LONGER TO BUILD A SNOWPIG THAN A SNOWBIRD?

You have to hollow the head out, first!

SHIVERY SIDE-SPLITTERS!

WHAT DO WOMEN USE TO STAY YOUNG LOOKING IN THE ARCTIC?

Cold cream!

WHAT SITS ON THE BOTTOM OF THE ARCTIC OCEAN AND SHAKES?

A nervous wreck.

WHAT DO PENGUINS EAT FOR LUNCH?

Ice-burgers!

HOW DO YOU AVOID GETTING COLD FEET?

Don't go around brrr-footed!

WHY AREN'T PENGUINS AS LUCKY AS THE ANGRY BIRDS?

The poor old penguins can't go south for the winter!

HOW DO YOU KNOW IF THERE'S A SNOWMAN IN YOUR BED?
You wake up with a cold!

WHAT DO YOU CALL FIFTY PENGUINS IN THE ARCTIC?
Lost! (They live in the Antarctic!)

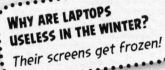

WHY ARE LAPTOPS USELESS IN THE WINTER?
Their screens get frozen!

KNOCK, KNOCK!
Who's there?
FREEZE.
Freeze who?
FREEZE A JOLLY GOOD FELLOW!

WHAT DID THE POLICE OFFICER SAY WHEN HE SAW JACK FROST STEALING?
Freeze!

SNOWY TWEETS

WHAT'S BLACK, WHITE, BLACK, WHITE, BLACK, WHITE, BLACK, WHITE?

A penguin rolling down a hill!

WHY DO PENGUINS CARRY FISH IN THEIR BEAKS?

Because they haven't got any pockets.

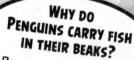

KNOCK, KNOCK!

Who's there?

KEN.

Ken who?

KEN I STAY HOME FROM SCHOOL TODAY? IT'S TOO COLD TO GO OUTSIDE!

SEASON'S GREED-INGS

HOW DID THE PIGS SCARE THE SNOWMAN?
They showed it a hairdryer!

WHAT DO YOU CALL SANTA WHEN HE STOPS MOVING?
Santa Pause!

HOW MUCH DID SANTA PAY FOR HIS SLEIGH?
Nothing, it was on the house!

WHY DO MUMMIES LIKE CHRISTMAS SO MUCH?
Because of all the wrapping!

WHY ARE CHRISTMAS TREES SUCH BAD KNITTERS?

They are always dropping their needles.

WHAT DID THE GHOST SING TO FATHER CHRISTMAS?

I'll have a boo Christmas without you.

WHAT DO THEY SING UNDER THE OCEAN IN DECEMBER?

Christmas corals!

WHAT DO YOU GET IF YOU CROSS MISTLETOE AND A DUCK?

A Christmas quacker!

WHERE DOES A SNOWMAN KEEP HIS MONEY?

In a snow bank!

WRECK THE HALLS!

WHAT IS INVISIBLE AND SMELLS LIKE MILK AND COOKIES?

Father Christmas's burps!

WHAT DO YOU CALL A SNOWMAN IN THE SUMMER?

A puddle!

WHAT IS YOUR PARENTS' FAVOURITE CHRISTMAS CAROL?

Silent Night.

WHAT NATIONALITY IS FATHER CHRISTMAS?

North Polish.

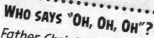

WHO SAYS "OH, OH, OH"?
Father Christmas walking backwards!

WHY DOES SANTA HAVE THREE GARDENS?
So he can hoe, hoe, hoe.

WHAT DO SNOWMEN EAT FOR BREAKFAST?
Frosted Flakes!

KING PIG: What's the best key to get at Christmas?

MINION: I don't know, great leader.

KING PIG: A turkey!

WHAT'S THE BEST THING TO GIVE YOUR PARENTS FOR CHRISTMAS?
A list of everything you want!

HO, HO, HO!

WHAT KIND OF BIRD CAN WRITE?
A pen-guin

WHY DID THE ELF PUSH HIS BED INTO THE FIREPLACE?
Because he wanted to sleep like a log!

WHAT DID THE CHRISTMAS TREE SAY TO THE PLUG?
You light me up!

WHAT DO YOU GET WHEN YOU EAT CHRISTMAS DECORATIONS?
Tinsilitis!

SEASONAL TWEETINGS

WHAT DO YOU GET IF YOU CROSS SANTA WITH A DETECTIVE?
Santa Clues!

WHAT DID ADAM SAY ON THE DAY BEFORE CHRISTMAS?
It's Christmas, Eve.

WHAT IS THE FEAR OF SANTA CLAUS CALLED?
Claus-trophobia

KNOCK, KNOCK!
Who's there?
SNOW.
Snow who?
SNOW USE - I'VE FORGOTTEN MY NAME AGAIN!

WHAT HAPPENED WHEN THE SNOWWOMAN GOT ANGRY AT THE SNOWMAN?
She gave him the cold shoulder.

HOW DOES GOOD KING WENCESLAS LIKE HIS PIZZAS?

Deep pan, crisp and even!

WHAT DO SANTA'S ELVES DO AFTER SCHOOL?

Their gnomework!

WHY DOES FATHER CHRISTMAS LIKE TO GO DOWN THE CHIMNEY?

Because it soots him!

RED: What's the difference between the Christmas alphabet and the normal alphabet?

HAL: Dunno!

RED: The Christmas alphabet has no L!

WHY IS IT COLD ON CHRISTMAS?

Because it's in Decem-brrr!